Contents

About Cats and Traveling

An Introduction

If you've ever tried to wrestle a cat into a carrier for a short trip to the vet, you may be very apprehensive about traveling with your cat. I completely understand! No one wants to open that can of worms, especially your poor cat. He just wants to peacefully relax at home and enjoy the pampered life that is a cat's right.

Unfortunately, sometimes a trip is necessary that is longer than what it takes to travel to your closest veterinarian. If you're moving to a new city or going on an extended vacation, you're not left with a lot of options. Making that dreaded trip with your cat in tow is inevitable.

On a positive note, traveling with a cat doesn't "need" to be a traumatic experience for either of you. This book will provide you with tips and strategies to make traveling with your cat much less stressful for you both. If you begin training when your cat is young (and sometimes even later in life) the training strategies and tips in this book may turn your cat into one of those rare felines who actually enjoys traveling by car.

Cats and Their Territory

Unlike dogs, whose sense of security comes from belonging to a pack (regardless of whether the pack is human or canine), a cat's sense of security comes from its territory. In their established territory a cat feels safe and secure. He or she knows the lay of the land, what to expect and where to hide should the need arise. They are familiar with the sights, sounds, and smells around them. They know who enters their territory and whether these infiltrators are friends or foes.

When a cat is taken from its territory, his or her sense of safety disappears. They feel very vulnerable, agitated and stressed. Every sight, sound and smell is new to them. There is a potential threat around every corner. Even noises or smells that you can't sense yourself can be perceived by your cat as a threat to his or her well-being. This sensory overload dramatically increases the tension they feel.

This is why most cats hate to travel. Imagine you are sleeping peacefully, dreaming whatever cats dream, only to suddenly find yourself scooped up, placed in an unfamiliar prison cell – that moves! – and removed from everything that makes you feel safe. This is what traveling feels like to a cat that hasn't been trained to travel. What an unimaginable nightmare it must be for them.

Fortunately, there are many ways to make this experience much less traumatic, and even somewhat enjoyable for some cats. All it takes is a few simple steps and tricks that require very little on the part of the human caregiver, but can make all the difference to the cat.

Cats Hate Change

The other thing that makes travel so hard on cats is that by its nature, travel means change. Most cats abhor change! It is the scariest thing that could ever happen to a cat. Some cats hate change so much that even rearranging the furniture can cause them to panic, let alone moving them to a completely new territory. It doesn't have to be that way, though. There are things you, as a caregiver, can do to make change less chaotic for your cat.

With my cats, I have always changed things. Since they were kittens, we have constantly rearranged the furniture, moved the litter boxes to new locations at a moment's notice, and changed the location of food and water dishes regularly. This has helped our cats to become adaptable. If you have a kitten and would like to be able to travel easily with your cat, start young. If you teach your kitten that things may move around, change will be less stressful.

Moving things to new locations will not work for all cats. Some cats are just more easily set off than others. That's the nature of a feline. If your cat is not tolerant of change and you are planning a trip, try to keep the routine as close to "normal" as possible. If you feed your cat at a specific time each day, continue that on your trip. If you have a designated playtime, stick to it as closely as possible. Keeping to a routine that is familiar to your cat will go a long way to decreasing his or her stress during your trip, making it more enjoyable for both of you.

Safety First

Rules of the Road

To keep your cat safe during your trip, the next four "rules" should be followed.

Rule #1: Your cat must remain in a carrier while the vehicle is in motion. A cat running loose inside a moving vehicle is a danger to the cat, the driver, the passengers and anyone else who is sharing the road with you. If a bump or a noise scares your cat, she may end up scratching you in her panic. She may also end up getting in the way of the gas or brake pedals. This can lead to a catastrophe.

Rule #2: Never open the doors or windows while the cat is free in the vehicle, without the cat securely wearing a harness and the leash firmly in your hand. Should the cat bolt for the great outdoors, it is much easier to stop him when on a leash than to chase a terrified cat across the road.

Rule #3: Never leave your cat unattended in a vehicle. Ever! The temperature in a car can rise or plummet very rapidly, which can quickly lead to heat-stroke or hypothermia – both very deadly. Another risk is theft. If you leave your car with your pet in it and the windows down to promote air flow, your car and your pet are both at risk of being stolen.

In warm weather, if you absolutely must leave your cat in the vehicle while you stop for a quick break, park the car in the shade, leave the windows open, and keep your cat in his or her carrier. Don't be gone for long! Every minute your cat is in the car poses a serious risk of overheating. On a hot day the temperature in your car can climb to deadly levels in 10 minutes! Cats don't sweat like humans do and it is much more difficult for them to regulate their body temperature, especially when confined to a small space. In cold weather, wrap the carrier in extra blankets to keep it warm and well insulated.

Rule #4: Visit a veterinarian before you travel. You want to make sure that your cat is fit enough for travel and that any precautions are taken care of in advance. See the chapter "Preparing for the Unexpected" for more information.

Preventing Escapes and Runaways

In the event that your cat should somehow escape from the vehicle, an ID tag with your cat's name and your phone number (at the very least) should be secured to a collar, or better yet, a harness, worn by the cat at all times during travel. In the unfortunate event that your cat escapes your vehicle, this will help him be returned to you, should someone find him.

Don't forget to take lots of photos of your cat before your trip! A recent photo showing your cat's unique markings may help immensely if your cat gets lost. Make sure the photos are clear and detailed. If you have a smartphone, that's perfect, but if not, make sure you get a print copy made of at least two photos of your cat before your trip. A side view and a front view are best. Also, aim for photos that really highlight any distinguishing features your cat may have – for example, a notched ear, an interestingly shaped patch of different coloured fur, a spot on her toe, or the freckles around his eyes. Photos taken in natural lighting are the best – find a sunny window and get a couple of good shots.

Another newer method of preventing the unexpected loss of a runaway pet is to invest in a tracking collar. These collars use GPS technology to track the location of your cat. These collars are relatively new to the market and may still need some fine-tuning. Many of them are rather bulky and some cats may not find them all too comfortable. Another downfall is that cats are adept at removing their collars, so the collar may be found, but not the cat. Depending on your cat and your situation this may be something worth looking into.

Microchipping is also a good idea, but will only help your pet be returned to you if the person who finds your cat takes him or her to a shelter or veterinarian to have the microchip scanned. Microchipping is safe. The chip is inserted under the cat's skin using a needle. It can be done at any time – anesthetic is not usually required. Once implanted, it can be scanned to bring up your contact information and help in returning your lost pet to you.

<u>Leash Training</u>

A crash course in leash training is a very good idea if your cat will be traveling. Even if you don't plan on traveling, learning to walk on a leash is a valuable skill for your cat to have.

It can take a while for a cat to become comfortable walking on a leash, but when a cat-guardian possesses a positive attitude, patience, perseverance and uses appropriate training techniques, I believe any cat can be trained. If you are planning to travel with your cat, it is best to start leash training as early as possible. From the first sight of the harness to walking happily beside you like a puppy can be a long journey.

As with any training exercise, when working with cats, you must start slowly and progress gradually. All cats will react differently the first time wearing a harness. Some cats will roll over and over again trying to move around because walking feels too difficult. Some will lie down and refuse to move at all. Some will desperately try to get the harness off. Eventually, if you keep putting the harness on your cat for short periods of time, the cat will become accustomed to the feel of the harness and will start to walk around normally. This is all you really need for a car trip. It's a safety measure, not a walk around the block.

Training a cat to do anything requires patience and dedication. If you want a fully leash-trained cat, I've written another book about leash training, which includes all the steps and measures you need to take to make walking your cat on a leash a very positive adventure. <u>Make sure you check it out!</u>

Pre-Trip Planning

Choosing Carrier Style and Size

With so many options available, choosing the right carrier can be challenging. Should you get a zippered, soft-sided carrier, a hard, plastic carrier, or a barred, crate-style cage? How big is too big and how small is too small? Knowing how often you plan to travel with your cat and how long the trips will take makes choosing a size and style much easier.

First, let's discuss the three styles of carriers mentioned above. Soft-sided carriers, with their zippered closures, can be dangerous. Not only do they not provide any sort of protection in the event that something falls on the carrier, but I've seen many cats figure out rather quickly how to undo those zippers and escape. For short trips, these carriers may be sufficient, as they're easy to store when not in use, but they're not the best choice for long trips. The last thing you want is for your cat to undo the zipper of his or her carrier and end up by your feet while you're driving!

Barred, crate-style cages (think dog crates) are another option when choosing a carrier, but they may also not be such a great choice, depending on you, your vehicle and your cat. I've found that most cats do not like them as they lack the sense of security that an enclosed carrier provides. Dog crates are an especially poor choice if your vehicle is not air conditioned. A dog crate, combined with the wind coming through open windows, is a sure-fire way to stress a cat and make for a very loud, annoying trip.

The final option is a hard, plastic carrier. These carriers come in many sizes and are well ventilated, while still providing a feeling of security that is reminiscent of hiding in a cave. They are easily cleaned if your cat has an accident or if food or water is spilled in the carrier. They come with different door options, too. Carriers with a top door, in addition to a side door, are perfect for cats that fight getting into a carrier – you just open the top door and gently place the cat in, with little to no hassle. (If your cat fights, try gently covering his or her eyes with your hand, just enough so that she can't see, but doesn't feel restrained, either).

Now let's take a look at size. You don't want a huge carrier for a small pet, but you also don't want one that's too tiny to be comfortable.

If you're only going to be making short trips with your cat, such as the annual visit to the veterinarian, a smaller carrier should serve just fine. Just make sure that it's big enough to accommodate your full-grown cat, or else you may need to invest in a larger one as your cat gets older.

If you intend to make longer trips with your cat, you will want to invest in a slightly larger carrier. It must be large enough for your cat to be able to stand up and move about comfortably, but not too large – I'm not talking a dog crate big enough to fit a German Shepherd! You want to make sure that while your cat is able to move around comfortably, the carrier is still small enough to feel cave-like. This cave-like feeling is why cats love cardboard boxes so much.

If you have more than one cat, how well they get along on the average day will be your best indication as to whether or not they can travel in the same carrier. If they are best friends and sleep together regularly, you're all good. They will most likely feel calmer and happier with each other to snuggle with. Make sure that the carrier you choose is large enough to accommodate both of them.

If your cats have shown any aggression or indifference toward each other, separate carriers may be the best option. It is better to have an extra carrier than two cats fighting the whole way to your destination and sometimes the stress of a trip can make even the best of friends fight.

One more important note before we move on: cardboard boxes or plastic totes are not a safe item to use as a cat carrier! Whichever style you choose, always make sure your cat is secure in an appropriate carrier when traveling.

<u>Making the Carrier Feel Comfy and Cozy</u>

Now that you've picked the size and style of carrier that best suits your cat's needs, let's talk about making it a comfy place for your cat to spend the day.

The key to making your cat feel safe in the carrier is to make it a warm and inviting place for your cat to be, not something scary. You want the carrier to feel like home and like a safe, comfortable nest. You want your cat to feel relaxed, not trapped.

Blankets and/or pillows are essential to the comfort of the carrier, but not just any blankets or pillows will do. When at all possible, you want to use your cat's favourite things to make the carrier feel as much like home as possible. Does your cat have a blanket that he or she sleeps on a lot? If so, use it! If not, and if you have some time before your trip, leave out some items that you feel would be good to use in the carrier and let your cat decide which ones he or she likes best.

Scent is very important here! You want to fill the carrier with things that smell like him – things he's marked as his. The longer your cat has "owned" the item, the better. Don't wash the blankets or pillows before your trip.

If there are no items that carry your cat's scent, rub her down with the items you want to use in the carrier every day before your trip. Pay special attention to her cheeks – cats have scent glands in their cheeks for marking territory and most cats love to have their cheeks and chin rubbed.

Another thing that you can use to make the carrier feel comfortable is your cat's favourite toys. Cloth toys are better for this than plastic ones, as the toys will soak up his or her scent, too. Although your cat may not play with these toys during the trip, it will make him feel safer to have them with him.

When putting blankets and pillows in the carrier, you want to make sure that the materials you use are not going to slip and slide when you turn a corner. You can use sticky-back Velcro attached to a pillow or a mat with a rubber bottom and the blankets piled on top to stop this.

Finally, you want to make sure that the carrier meets the "softness" needs of your cat. For short trips, this isn't so important, but for long ones it can make all the difference. If your cat prefers to sleep on the couch, try to make the bottom of the carrier as close to the softness of your couch as possible. If your cat prefers to sleep on harder surfaces, she may prefer less pillows or blankets. You know your cat best! Try to make the carrier as comfortable as you can.

Making the Carrier Feel Safe and Secure

There are two parts to this section: the first is making your cat "feel" safe; the second is making certain that your cat "is" secure in his or her carrier.

To make your cat feel safe in his or her carrier, he or she must have had positive experiences with a carrier in the past. If your cat has had negative experiences with a carrier, retraining your cat to like a carrier is possible, but it will take a lot of time.

The first step to training or retraining a cat to enjoy being in a carrier is to have access to it. I highly recommend, even if you don't intend to travel with your cat regularly, that a carrier be left in a place where it can be accessed by your cat any time he or she wants to escape into it. If your cat has not had experiences with a carrier yet, the carrier becomes an inviting "safe-zone". If your cat has had bad experiences, start slowly and praise your cat with his or her favourite things (petting, treats, play) every time he or she makes progress towards accepting the carrier. Once your cat has decided that it likes this cozy, safe place you've provided, any issues the cat has had with carriers before should not occur again. If you have to force your cat into a carrier again, this will create stress and will undo any progress that has been achieved. Patience is essential when working with cats.

Now your cat "feels" safe in her carrier, but are you really sure she is? There are a few very important things you must do to make sure your cat is as safe as possible.

The first and most important safety measure is to check the doors! I arrived at my veterinarian's office one day to find the veterinarian and three of his staff running around the parking lot and the surrounding streets. A cat had escaped from its carrier and they were trying to find it while the owner was panicking and at a loss as to how this happened. When the cat had finally been recovered (and was safe, thank goodness), I asked my vet what had happened. There was a front and back door on this particular carrier. He had checked the door he took the cat out of to make sure it was firmly closed when he put her back in the carrier to go home, but he didn't think to check the other door. It wasn't securely closed. When the owner picked up the carrier and the cat's weight made it tip backwards slightly, the door burst open and the cat ran, completely terrified to find herself suddenly out in the open.

To prevent a similar situation from happening to you, especially when traveling with no one else around to help, make sure that you check all doors and clips on the carrier every time you use it. If something is missing or not functioning properly, it's time for the carrier to be replaced. Using a damaged carrier poses a serious risk to your cat.

Another important safety precaution is using seatbelts. Although it can be difficult to buckle a carrier into your car, it is a very important thing to do. You want your cat to be just as safe as you are. Practicing a few times with an empty carrier can be a lot easier than trying to buckle in a crying, upset cat.

If it's not possible to use a seatbelt to buckle in your cat's carrier, you want to make sure that the carrier is placed where it will not slip or slide around. Any sudden movement, like slamming on the brakes, can make a carrier slide around. This will scare your cat and may damage his opinion of the rest of the trip. Make sure it's tucked snugly in place and not likely to move around.

Your cat will also feel much happier and safer if the carrier is placed somewhere where he or she can see you. Being able to see you is reassuring, even if your cat doesn't show it.

Preventing "Accidents" in the Carrier

Many people worry about their cat having an "accident" while in the carrier. In normal situations, this is highly unlikely to occur, even with young kittens on long drives. It is more likely to occur if you have a very stressed or ill cat. A test run before your journey should prepare you for how your cat will behave in a vehicle.

If you want to make clean up easier, just in case, I recommend bringing along extra blankets and lining the bottom of the carrier with absorbent puppy training pads. It is a very good idea to have extra blankets on hand in the event of spills or motion sickness, too (see "Preparing for the Unexpected" for more information).

Water spills very easily in a moving vehicle, and your cat is going to hate being splashed, not to mention sleeping on wet blankets. It is in your cat's best interests not to provide food or water while the vehicle is in motion. More tips about feeding and providing water on long trips are coming up in the chapter on "Long Car Trips".

Training with Mini-Trips

If you know ahead of time you will be traveling, it is a good idea to get your cat accustomed to traveling by car. Not only will this ease the stress on your cat, but it will help you determine if your cat is afflicted by motion sickness, has bowel or bladder incontinence when in a vehicle, or yowls up a storm in the car and will help you to prepare for these circumstances before your real trip.

The following process for carrier training should be taken very slowly. Follow your cat's lead. Don't rush things. If you move too fast, you will experience setbacks. Wait until you are sure your cat is 100 percent comfortable before moving onto the next step.

You should begin taking your cat on mini trips as soon as he is comfortable entering the carrier by himself, calmly, without being forced. Start off by placing your cat in the carrier and then into the car. Do not turn the car on at this point. Just let your cat smell the new surroundings and check out the new sights. You can also let your cat wander around the car (but keep it turned off) to really get a good feel for it and begin to claim it as his or her territory.

After your cat is comfortable in the car, you can repeat the same process, but this time with the car turned on. It's probably unnecessary to allow your cat out of the carrier during this and the following steps, as your cat should never roam free in the car while you're driving. After your cat is comfortable in a running vehicle, you can then progress to short trips around the block. Let your cat set the pace of progress. If he or she seems uncomfortable or begins to show signs of stress, end the trip for the day and try again another day. Gradually increase the length of time your cat spends in the vehicle and your cat will become more accustomed to traveling for longer periods of time.

It is very strange for a cat to be in a vehicle. The sense of motion can play with their senses and it's a new feeling for them that may be extremely uncomfortable. If you want your cat to enjoy car rides, taking it slow is the best way to accomplish this. Once your cat is comfortable on short trips across town, long trips should be a breeze from this point on.

Reducing Stress

Don't Get Caught Unprepared

I know you're busy packing for yourself and any other humans that are going on this trip with you, but don't forget to pack a bag for your cat, too. He or she doesn't need much, but you'll want to make sure you have all of the essentials and a few extras on hand.

Try to avoid sample-sized packages of food unless it is what your cat is already eating. Routine and as little change as possible is what you're aiming for. It is also a very good idea to pack some jugs of the water your cat has been drinking at home. Cats are known to be finicky and some may not drink "strange" water. As convenient as travel-sized food and water dishes may be, your cat will much prefer eating and drinking from his or her regular dishes. Try to bring all the comforts of home with you to ease your cat's stress.

Many sources recommend bringing disposable litter boxes, and with some cats, this may be a very handy solution. On the other hand, if there's one thing most cats are picky about, it's their litter boxes. If at all possible, bring your cat's normal litter box and use the same litter you always use. If the regular litter box is too bulky for travel, allow your cat some time to adjust to using your preferred "travel box" before your trip. It may make a huge difference! You'll also need to bring bags to dispose of dirty litter and feces and a litter scoop, too.

Your cat will probably greatly appreciate it if you bring along his or her favourite toys and maybe even some catnip, too. (See the section called "Calming Kitty Down" in this chapter for more information about catnip.) Toys such as feather wands are great to use in a parked vehicle for your cat to get some exercise, so bring one of those along, too. (More information on playing during a trip can be found in the chapter "Long Car Trips".

Lastly, you'll want to make sure you have any medications that your cat may need (talk to your vet before giving anything new or non-prescribed to your cat). Bring along a first-aid kit, as well, if you don't already have one in your vehicle. It could be very bad if your cat ended up injured and you didn't have anything on hand.

Your cat really doesn't need much, but preparing ahead of time and making sure that everything your cat could possibly need is within easy reach will decrease your stress as well as the stress on your cat.

<u>Don't Drink and Drive</u>

I'm not going to give you a lecture about driving under the influence (although you shouldn't drink and drive). Instead, I want to give you my advice about providing food and water before and during short road trips. Long trips are a bit different, but we'll talk about that in a later chapter.

If your drive is less than six hours, you don't need to worry about providing food or water for your cat during the ride – he or she probably won't be interested in it anyway. Feed your cat three to five hours before your trip. You can continue to offer water right up until your cat gets in the carrier and you begin your adventure. If you feed your cat right before the trip, it may lead to messy situations when a full stomach is combined with stress and motion sickness.

Many carriers come with food and water dishes that can be attached to the carrier. These probably aren't such a good idea to use. Your cat is really not likely to be hungry or even thirsty during a short trip (up to six hours) and placing food and water in the carrier is most likely to result in a mess and a wet cat who is angrier than she was before you offered her something to eat and drink.

If your drive is longer than six hours, please see the chapter entitled "<u>Long Car Trips</u>" for tips on providing food and water in a vehicle.

Making Conversation

Traveling with a cat would be so much easier if cats enjoyed car rides like most dogs do. Unfortunately, instead of sticking his or her head out the window and enjoying every second of the trip, your cat is more likely to yowl and cry and make sure you know how unhappy he or she is. The noise will probably drive you crazy, but your cat is not suffering. She's just voicing her displeasure the only way she knows how.

Talking to your cat in a soft, soothing voice can make a world of difference. It is reassuring for a cat to hear her owner talking in a calm manner. As annoyed and frustrated as you may get if your cat is one of the noisy ones, do your best to refrain from talking to him or her in a harsh, angry tone. This will only make the problem worse.

Depending on the length of your trip, hopefully your cat will quiet down after a while, relax, close her eyes and fall asleep.

<u>Serenading Your Cat</u>

Most people listen to music of some sort while travelling in a vehicle. It's just a thing we humans do. This shouldn't bother your cat too much, especially if music is played regularly around your home. With the right music (something familiar to your cat) and the right volume, it may even help your cat relax.

On the other hand, cats have extremely sensitive hearing. Although your music may not seem loud to you, it will be twice as loud, if not louder, for your cat. In a home, a cat can escape to a quieter room if the music is painful to listen to, but within a carrier in a vehicle this is not possible. I don't know if cats get headaches, but I know if I listen to music too loudly for too long, I certainly do.

It is because of this that I do not recommend trying to drown out your cat's cries by turning up the volume. If the loud music is causing your cat pain and distress, it will only make your cat cry louder to get your attention, defeating the purpose of turning up the volume in the first place and reinforcing why your cat hates car rides.

When in a vehicle with a cat, try to keep the music low. Also, aim for music that will not be upsetting to the cat, if at all possible. Cats can hear sounds that we can't, so if your cat begins to cry during a song, he or she may be hearing something that you can't and it may not be to his or her liking. If your cat reacts this way, it's probably best for everyone involved to skip to another song.

<u>Feeling the Breeze in Her Fur</u>

Have you ever had the experience of your ears becoming stuffed when the wind is blowing in an open window while driving at highway speed? If you have, you know how uncomfortable that sensation can be. Imagine how your cat would feel with those big ears designed to funnel sound deep inside. It must be incredibly painful.

My daughter was riding in the backseat of a car the other day with the windows open. She mentioned that the wind coming in the windows was making it slightly difficult for her to breathe. This is not an uncommon complaint from backseat passengers. Whether you place the carrier in the front or back seat, keep in mind that it may be difficult for your cat to breathe normally with the windows open. Your cat can't tell you how he or she is feeling. Difficulty breathing would certainly cause your cat stress, especially when he or she can't escape the situation. When possible, drive with the windows closed!

One of my cats once really enjoyed car rides, or at the very least, tolerated them without complaint. She travelled quite a bit. Then, one day, I had a friend bring her home, and they had to make do with a dog kennel. They also owned a Jeep. After that trip home, she has never been the same in a vehicle. She hates them. The only thing that was different was the wind in the vehicle, as we always travel with the windows closed.

It's unfortunate, but a cat that was a great traveler turned into a cat that hates vehicles due to one short trip. This is why I highly recommend that if at all possible, you keep the windows closed while traveling with a cat in the car. If this is not possible, make certain that you are using a hard, plastic carrier and cover the carrier with a blanket if necessary.

Calming Kitty Down

You want your cat to be as relaxed as possible during your trip, both for your cat's well-being and your own peace of mind. There are products available that help immensely in these situations. The most well-known of these products, called Comfort Zone with Feliway, uses synthetic pheromones to help calm a cat down. This product is most commonly seen in a diffuser, which doesn't help much in a vehicle. Luckily it is also available in a convenient spray.

Comfort Zone with Feliway is non-toxic and works only on cats. You won't be able to smell it at all and it won't bother a dog if you're traveling with one, too.

Simply spray Comfort Zone on the inside of the carrier and/or the blankets and bedding approximately five to ten minutes before you want your cat to go into the carrier. Once your cat is in the carrier, it shouldn't take long for the calming effect of the pheromones to start working. As with anything new, it's a good idea to test your cat's reaction to this product before your trip, so there are no unexpected surprises.

Comfort Zone is intended to be used on inanimate objects only. Please do not spray it directly on your cat or any other animals. Depending on the cat, sometimes you can get away with spraying it on the cat's collar, but you shouldn't need to go that far. If you do spray it on his collar, please take the collar off, spray it down, and then put it back on.

In addition to or instead of Comfort Zone with Feliway you may also use catnip to distract and calm your cat. Every cat reacts differently, so make sure you know how your cat reacts to catnip before using it in the carrier. If your cat is the type to run around wildly, chasing imaginary prey and causing a ruckus when given catnip, it may not be appropriate to give it to him during your trip. You can use a spray, crushed leaves, or a ball of compressed catnip – whatever your cat likes best.

Sedatives and Tranquilizers

If your cat becomes very stressed during car rides and none of the other
suggestions in this book have helped to calm his nerves, you can request a
sedative, tranquilizer or anxiety-reducing medication from your veterinarian.

Do not try to medicate your cat without first consulting with a licensed
veterinarian. Many medications sold for human use are extremely harmful or
even deadly to pets. There are also enormous differences between dosages for
humans and animals.

Certain medications used with some cats can have an effect that is the
opposite of what was intended. For instance, some tranquilizers may cause
aggression in cats. If it all possible, it would be a good idea to test any
medication to see how your cat will react to it before you take a journey
beyond the reach of your trusted veterinarian. Medications your cat has never
taken before might cause unpleasant side-effects, just like in human
medication. At the very least, make sure you discuss all of the possibilities
and side-effects of any medication thoroughly with your veterinarian before
giving it to your cat.

Arriving at Your Destination

When you arrive at your destination, whether it be a new home you're moving into, a cottage you're spending the summer in, a winter retreat, a relative's home, or any other destination, you want to continue to keep your cat as calm and relaxed as possible. Your cat needs time to settle into his or her new surroundings and attempt to re-establish his or her territory.

This is where a safe room becomes important. It is best to confine your cat to one room while you unpack and settle in. Choose the room you think is best (bathrooms are usually an excellent choice). Before you begin setting up the room for your cat to explore, check and make sure that there's nothing that could be unsafe for your cat. Look for places where your cat could get trapped, or anything else that may be dangerous (such as pest traps).

It is extremely important to check the room thoroughly and make sure that there is no possible way for your cat to escape. The last time I moved, we lost a cat. There was a rip in one of our screens and when he found the hole, he fled. We searched for months and we were unable to find him. A few years later, while walking around our neighbourhood, we happened to see him, happily sleeping on someone else's porch. It was sad to lose him, but reassuring to know that he had found a safe and loving home. Don't let this happen to you!

To make the room you've chosen feel safe for your cat, put everything you have on hand that smells like home in the room to make it as familiar and comfortable as possible. Don't forget to put out food and water dishes and a clean litter box. After you've set up the room and checked that everything's safe, take the carrier straight into the room you've chosen, open the door to the carrier, and leave your cat alone to investigate in her own time.

Once your cat has had an hour or two to settle, don't forget to visit. She'll be happy to know that she has not been abandoned in this strange place. Play with her, cuddle and pet her. The more attention you can lavish on your cat, the more secure he or she will feel. Don't take it too far though – follow your cat's lead and know when she's had enough. It may take a few days for your cat to come around and start enjoying his or her new surroundings.

Want more information about moving to a new home while reducing the stress it places on your cat? Check out our website for more great books! The link can be found in the "About the Author" section.

Preparing for the Unexpected

<u>Motion Sickness</u>

The motion of a vehicle is not well tolerated by some cats and they may end up suffering from motion sickness. If your cat is one of these unlucky ones, refrain from feeding your cat any food or treats for a few hours before or during the trip. Water may or may not be tolerated. If your trip is a shorter one, you don't need to worry – your cat should be fine without food for one day.

If your pet is very young and suffers from motion sickness, you may want to keep some corn syrup or karo syrup on hand and offer some to him or her every few hours. Kittens can become hypoglycemic very quickly without food and the corn syrup will keep their sugar levels from dropping too low. Only offer tiny amounts as this may upset your kitten's tummy if she's already feeling nauseous.

If your cat has an illness that requires a regular feeding schedule, other dietary modifications or specific care instructions, make sure you discuss this with your veterinarian before your trip begins. Ask what you can do to make the trip as safe and comfortable as possible for your pet.

If your cat is prone to motion sickness, anti-nausea medications may be helpful. Your veterinarian can prescribe these for your cat. As mentioned earlier – never give your pet any medication without speaking to a licensed veterinarian first. If you do, you could inadvertently kill your beloved cat.

Sudden Illness or Injury

When planning your trip, you should make note of any emergency veterinary clinics along your route. Write down their phone number, address and business hours. In the event that your pet becomes ill during the trip, it's better to have this information on hand than to be scrambling to find an open clinic while you're worried about your pet.

Your veterinarian should also be able to provide you with a "Passport" that provides information on your cat's care needs and what treatments (including vaccinations) your cat has received in the past. It is a good idea to keep one of these passports on you when traveling. Start keeping one in kittenhood, if possible, and continue to update it every time your cat sees a vet. When you're traveling and an emergency occurs, this will provide the attending veterinarian with all of your cat's pertinent medical history.

Keep a first-aid-kit on hand as well. In the event that your cat pulls out a claw trying to escape from the carrier or otherwise ends up injured, you'll want to make sure that you have emergency equipment on hand to get your cat through until you can make it to the nearest veterinarian.

Make sure you find a veterinary clinic at your destination, too. It's always better to be safe than sorry.

Preventing Fleas

Fleas! Gross! No one wants to think about these disgusting, annoying little bugs while prepping for a relaxing getaway, but I promise you, you don't want to be dealing with them while you're away from home, either.

Unfortunately, fleas are a very common pest. In fact, they are so common they can be found almost anywhere on the globe. If your pet steps outside your vehicle for a second (when on a leash, of course) he or she may pick up a flea or two. It doesn't take long at all for one or two fleas to become an infestation! You also want to be protected if you're staying at a pet-friendly hotel – you don't know if the last person to stay in the same room with their cat or dog was as diligent as you are about keeping their pets healthy and safe.

Before you leave for your trip, make sure you visit your veterinarian for an effective flea-treatment. Spot treatments, such as Advantage, are easy to use and will protect your pet for up to a month (as long as he or she doesn't take a bath). Alternatively, you can take a flea shampoo with you to bathe your pet when you arrive at your destination (although you may end up with fleas in your car during the rest of the trip!). Be careful with pet and department store flea products – they may actually do more harm than good.

Talk to your veterinarian about the many flea-treatment options available and choose the one that feels right for you.

At the Border

If you will be crossing the border with your cat, you will need to make sure you have the appropriate documentation on hand, just in case you're asked to provide it. The passport mentioned earlier is a very useful piece of paper, but it may not be enough for a border crossing.

This is one reason why a pre-trip visit to your veterinarian is crucial to your trip. To cross the border between Canada and the United States, a pet must be vaccinated against rabies, and sometimes other core vaccines are also required. You may be asked to show proof of up-to-date vaccinations. If you're crossing a border with your cat, make sure you check into required vaccines and what documentation must be provided. Every state or province may have different requirements. Research the requirements for all the areas you're traveling to or through before you go.

It is also a good idea to have your vet sign a declaration stating that the cat is in good health and free from infectious diseases to the best of their knowledge. Most vets have no issues providing you with such a document and it may save your cat from being quarantined, which could really disrupt your plans.

Long Car Trips – Over Six Hours in Duration

Providing Food and Water

Although your cat will be fine without food or water for a few hours, if your trip is longer than a six to eight hour drive, your cat will need to eat or at the very least have a sip of water. Here are a few guidelines you should follow when offering food and water on a long car ride:

1. Don't feed your cat in his or her carrier. This will make a mess! Your cat will be very unhappy if he or she has to sleep on soaking wet blankets. In a car a water dish is going to spill – I can almost guarantee it. A treat or two is fine if your cat wants to eat it, but save meals for when you're stopped.

Instead of offering food or water to your cat in his or her carrier, place the food and water dishes on the floor of your car and allow your cat freedom from the carrier for a few minutes. Only do this when your car is parked! If hungry or thirsty, your cat will not pass up the opportunity for a snack.

2. Don't offer food or water while the car is in motion. No cat is going to eat while he or she feels uncomfortable and the motion of a vehicle is upsetting to most cats. When you stop for a bite to eat or a bathroom break, allow your cat the opportunity to refresh himself as well. You'll likely find he or she is much more willing to eat when the car is parked.

3. Always aim for consistency. During your trip, continue to offer your cat the same food he or she eats at home. Keeping things as similar as possible to home will reduce your cat's stress. Also, many cats suffer from digestive upset (and vomiting) when their food is switched. The last thing you want is for your cat to have an upset tummy on your trip.

Your cat may also appreciate it if you bring some jugs or bottles of the water he's familiar with drinking from home. Many cats will not drink water that tastes strange – it's a survival mechanism (and just plain pickiness).

Remember – for safety's sake, your cat should always be wearing a harness and leash when outside his or her carrier. Be careful that the leash does not get caught on anything. This could upset your cat and cause him or her to panic.

Bathroom Breaks – Using the Litter Box

When possible, try to make sure your cat has used his or her litter box before the trip begins. To accomplish this, you can close your cat in a small room, such as a bathroom, for an hour or so before you leave. You can't force your cat to use his litter box, and he may not. Either way, unless he or she has problems with his bowel or bladder, your cat should be able to hold it for a few hours.

If your trip is a long one, your cat will need to pee at some point. Allow your cat the freedom to use the litter box when you stop for a bathroom break yourself. Set up a litter box on the floor of your vehicle and allow your cat to roam freely in the car for a few minutes (with the windows and doors all closed). If your cat really needs to go, he or she will find the litter box and use it. Just make sure you dispose of the mess before continuing your drive or it will stink up your car very quickly.

Having some of your favourite air freshener on hand is a good idea, too. No one wants to be trapped in a vehicle after a cat has just made it rather smelly.

If your cat doesn't use the litter box, keep trying every few hours. He may or may not use it on the trip, especially if he's not eating or drinking. When you stop for the night or arrive at your destination, she'll probably want to use it then, so it should be one of the first things you set up.

Disposable litter boxes are handy, but your cat may refuse to use an unfamiliar box. As mentioned earlier, try to keep the litter box as similar to the one he or she has at home as possible. Cats don't generally like things that seem different.

Getting Some Exercise

Do you get stiff and need to stretch when sitting in a car for long periods of time? Your cat probably does, too (even though she's hopefully spent the entire trip sleeping peacefully). Once or twice a day, you should let your cat out of the carrier for some playtime and snuggles. Make sure your cat is wearing a harness (and leash, when possible) every time he or she is not in the carrier.

Close all the doors and windows in the vehicle and allow your cat to roam freely. If she wants to sit on your lap, snuggle and reassure her for a few minutes. Your touch will help ease any stress she may be feeling.

Feather wands are great toys for letting your cat get some exercise in a small space. He or she should be able to stalk and pounce on the feather wand and can use the seats and floors to his or her advantage while doing so. It may just be one of the most entertaining playtimes yet!

Be careful while your cat is roaming free in the vehicle that he or she does not get stuck under a seat or wedged into another place a little too tight for comfort. If your cat is afraid of the vehicle, it's probably best to keep him or her in the carrier until you reach your destination. Also, keep a close eye on those doors and windows! You don't want your cat to escape if you accidently open the window by placing your elbow on the button or if someone traveling with you suddenly opens a door. Safety first!

If you're staying the night in a hotel, once you've settled into your room, take advantage of this fantastic time to release some of your cat's pent up energy from the long drive.

A good play session leaves a cat too tired to play any longer. Keep it up as long as you can!

Pet-Friendly Hotels

If traveling to your destination takes several days and you don't plan to sleep in your vehicle, you will want to look into pet-friendly hotels along your route. Fortunately, there are many of these accommodations available.

When booking your stay, make sure you call the hotel ahead of time to let them know that you will be bringing a cat with you and inquire about their pet policy. Unfortunately, many "pet-friendly" hotels are really only "dog-friendly" and you don't want to be surprised when you arrive to find out that pets don't include cats. Get the name of the person with whom you are making the reservation, and if at all possible, get confirmation in writing that states your cat is welcome to stay the night, too.

Don't try to sneak into the hotel with your cat hidden in your suitcase. If your cat cries you may be caught and kicked out of the hotel. The last thing you want is to be scrambling around an unfamiliar city in the dead of night looking for a place for you and your cat to sleep. The right hotel, if they know you're coming, will not have a problem with your cat spending the night with you.

You may be asked to place a security deposit when staying in a hotel with a cat. This is to protect the hotel in the event that your cat causes damage to the room or its furniture. If your cat enjoys scratching furniture or carpets, or is otherwise destructive, the bathroom is probably the best place for her to spend the night.

You may want to keep your cat confined to one room for the night, anyway. Cats don't generally like strange places and having only one room to explore and claim will make your cat settle into the new environment faster. On the other hand, only you know your cat best – he or she may prefer the comfort and security of sleeping curled up with you, instead of locked up where he or she can't see, hear and smell you.

Always thoroughly check for hazards in any new place. Make sure there's nowhere your cat can get trapped. Check for holes that could allow your cat to escape. Be on the lookout for poisons (such as ant-traps) and other unsafe objects. When you're sure the room is safe for your cat, set up his or her litter box, food dishes and bedding and then allow him or her freedom from the carrier.

Before checking out of your room make sure you check to see if your cat has caused any damage or hidden a favourite toy behind the bed. You wouldn't want to forget anything or be surprised by the hotel withholding your security deposit due to damages.

Alternative Options

Traveling by Air or Train

Sometimes, traveling by car just isn't possible, but there are other options to get your cat safely to your destination.

When traveling by plane, you may have two options: your cat can travel in the cargo hold, or sometimes with you in the cabin. If the cabin is an option with the airline you've chosen, this is a much better choice as far as your cat is concerned. Although flying is very stressful, it is much less so in the cabin than in the cargo hold.

Most airlines limit the number of cats that can travel in the cabin on any given flight. Make sure you book your flight well in advance and arrive at the airport early on the day of travel. Most airlines also add a surcharge for pets. This is usually more expensive when bringing your cat in the cabin with you, but well worth it for safety's sake and peace of mind.

When traveling in the cabin the carrier must be quite small. If you have a large cat, he or she may have to travel in the cargo hold, just to accommodate the size of the carrier. Make sure you look carefully into the airline's carrier regulations and their pet policies before booking your flight.

Sedatives or tranquilizers may be needed during a flight with a cat. Consult with your veterinarian beforehand.

Always withhold food the night before and morning of your flight to prevent your cat from vomiting during the trip. You don't want your cat to spend the flight in a messy, uncomfortable space. You want her to be as calm and relaxed as possible.

When traveling by train, your cat must ride in the baggage car. Baggage cars can reach extremely high temperatures in the summer months, and because of this, many trains do not permit pets on board during hot weather. If you're traveling by train in colder weather, inquire about the temperatures in the baggage cars and provide your cat with extra blankets if necessary.

As with airlines, train stations have strict guidelines in regards to the size and style of carrier permitted. Always make sure that the carrier you've chosen meets these guidelines – if you don't, your cat may not be permitted to travel. Many train stations offer carrier rentals for traveling pets.

Additional fees apply to cats traveling by train, as well.

Boarding Your Cat

If you're going on a short vacation and will be returning, it may be better for your cat to stay at a boarding facility rather than travel with you.

Boarding facilities come in many variations. Some accept dogs and cats, while others are species specific. If your cat has never been introduced to dogs or is known to be afraid of them, seeking a cat-only boarding facility will greatly reduce his or her stress.

The size of the cages or pens that animals are kept in will differ from one facility to another. Some offer luxury suites, including lots of space, ledges for perching and sometimes even a window. Others offer only small cages with food, water, a litter box and a bed. Take a tour of all the options in your area before committing to one. Choose what's best for your cat and your budget. While you're there, make sure you check for the cleanliness of the pens and observe the health of any cats that are currently staying there, too.

Most boarding facilities will require that your cat be up-to-date on all core vaccines as well as being flea treated and dewormed beforehand. If vaccinations are not required, for the safety of your cat I would highly recommend that you look for somewhere else to board your cat.

If your cat suffers from an illness or other medical condition, many veterinary clinics also offer boarding. Having your cat stay with a veterinarian ensures that your cat is taken care of by professionals and is in the best hands should his or her illness worsen while you're away.

Keep in mind that many boarding facilities are not monitored at night. If your cat is healthy, this should not be a problem. If your cat suffers from an illness, you may want to look for a facility that is staffed at night.

Hiring a Cat Sitter

If you're returning home after your trip, hiring a cat sitter is the best option insofar as your cat is concerned. Your cat gets to remain in the comfort of his or her own territory. Although you will miss your cat, it is much better for him or her to stay home whenever possible.

A friend, relative or neighbour is usually the best choice. They are likely already familiar with your cat and your home and you probably trust them.

If you do not have friends or family that can look after your cat while you're away, cat sitters are the next best option. You can find cat sitters just about everywhere – check classified ads, ask your veterinarian, or ask friends and/or coworkers for recommendations. Always get references!

Some cat sitters are professionals and are bonded and insured. Although they are likely to be slightly more expensive than ones who are not, you will have peace of mind knowing that you're protected if something goes wrong.

A cat sitter doesn't need to move into your home while you're away. They should come at least once, preferably twice, each day to check on your cat. It is the cat sitter's job to not only feed and water your cat and change his or her litter box, but also to play with and provide companionship for your cat. If it's too much work for one person, there's no harm in asking more than one of your friends or family members to help out.

<u>Shipping Your Cat</u>

Lastly, if you're moving or taking an extended vacation, you may ship your cat to your destination. There are many companies with experience in shipping pets. Their experience may be in local shipping, across continents or anything in between.

Each destination will have different requirements and regulations when shipping live animals. Your cat may also have to spend up to a month in quarantine if entering certain countries. You will need to thoroughly look into these regulations before shipping your cat. The company you have chosen to work with to ship your cat should be able to provide you with all of the necessary information and tips to reduce your cat's stress during shipping.

Please keep in mind that shipping a cat is extremely stressful for them. It should only be used if all other options are not practical. Don't forget to read reviews about other pet guardians' experiences with a company before choosing a shipping service.